THE RADIO CITY
CHRISTMAS
SPECTACULAR

THE RADIO CITY
CHRISTMAS SPECTACULAR

MELCHER
MEDIA

MSG
ENTERTAINMENT

Published by
Melcher Media, Inc.
124 West 13th Street
New York, NY 10011
www.melcher.com

In association with Madison Square Garden Entertainment

Publisher: Charles Melcher
Associate Publisher: Bonnie Eldon
Editor in Chief: Duncan Bock
Executive Editor: Lia Ronnen
Production Director: Kurt Andrews
Project Editor: Lindsey Stanberry

Design by Naomi Mizusaki, Supermarket

Photography credits, constituting an extension of the copyright page,
appear on page 148.

08 09 10 11 12   10 9 8 7 6 5 4 3 2 1

ISBN: 978-1-59591-050-9

Printed in the United States

TABLE OF CONTENTS

The 1964 finale of the *Radio City Christmas Spectacular*.

The expectant crowds settle into their red velvet seats. The glorious curtain is set to rise. The historic auditorium is lit like a sunset over the ocean. This is the scene before every *Radio City Christmas Spectacular.*

It happens up to six times a day, seven days a week during the holiday season, but each and every time the curtain rises, something truly unique and special happens: a one-of-a-kind show takes to the stage.

Decades of history, and the work of hundreds of performers, designers, directors, and choreographers, are brought to life with every performance of the *Radio City Christmas Spectacular*.

This is a celebration of the most popular live holiday show in the world. It is the history of Radio City Music Hall, the Radio City Rockettes, and the 90-minute spectacular that has entertained millions of people over the last eight decades. It is a chance to go behind-the-scenes to see just how the show is created, from the stunning sets to the impressive choreography. And it is a collection of the show's most treasured scenes, from the "Parade of the Wooden Soldiers" to the "Living Nativity."

Here is the chance to spend a little more time with the Rockettes, and Santa, and the thrill of the *Radio City Christmas Spectacular*!

WELCOME TO THE SHOW!

Radio City Music Hall decorated for the holiday season, 1999.

CHAPTER ONE

SHOWPLACE OF THE NATION

FOR MILLIONS OF PEOPLE, the holiday season wouldn't be the same without a trip to Radio City Music Hall to see the *Radio City Christmas Spectacular*. What many visitors don't know is how much this perennial New York tradition has changed over the years. In 1932, the grand theater rose on Sixth Avenue as a beacon of hope and progress during the bleak period of the Great Depression. And the tradition known as the *Radio City Christmas Spectacular* debuted a year after the Music Hall opened, starring the Rockettes, the precision dance company that would eventually become a symbol of Radio City itself.

ROXY'S MASTERPIECE: BUILDING RADIO CITY MUSIC HALL

In October 1928, in the midst of a booming economy, John D. Rockefeller Jr. signed a lease for a sizable swath of land in midtown Manhattan. The majority of the property was to be used for a new Metropolitan Opera House. But when the stock market crashed in the fall of 1929, plans for the opera house quickly unraveled, and Rockefeller elected instead to build a city within a city—the constellation of buildings now known as Rockefeller Center.

A view of Radio City Music Hall, before the high-rises of midtown Manhattan grew up around it.

One section of the land Rockefeller developed ran along Sixth Avenue, which at the time was a far cry from the gleaming corridor of culture and commerce that it is today. The strip was undesirable. The solution was to build a theater on the property and construct an enormous sign so big it would be visible from the theater district several blocks to the south.

The first building in the complex to make its debut was the space initially referred to in architectural plans as Theater No. 10, which later became known as Radio City Music Hall. Featuring the block-long, six-story Grand Foyer, a ceiling that soared to an apex of 84 feet, more than 6,000 seats, and a magnificent 144-foot-by-66-foot stage, the theater was an architectural marvel and the first of its kind.

Eager to establish the theater as the world's greatest entertainment venue (it would be, after all, the world's largest), Rockefeller enlisted the producing talents of renowned showman Samuel "Roxy" Rothafel, an entertainment impresario who had made his name in show business by revitalizing vaudeville theaters across America.

The job of designing the interior of the theater was awarded to Donald Deskey, the underdog candidate, who winningly presented his art deco concept with examples of the artisans' work he would incorporate in his design.

Long before any acts graced the Radio City stage, Roxy served as a creative force behind many design aspects of the theater, from aesthetic details to architectural elements that are now part of the Music Hall's signature look. The moving stage powered by cutting-edge hydraulics, the graduated choral staircases, the cantilevered mezzanines providing unobstructed views, and the great sculptured curtain (the largest in the world) are all part of Roxy's vision. Perhaps most notably, Roxy conceived the design of Radio City's trademark arched ceiling, constructed to ensure optimal acoustics and, as legend has it, mimic a sunset Roxy once enjoyed from the deck of an ocean liner crossing the Atlantic.

Earlier in his career, Roxy encountered a troupe of precision dancers dubbed the Missouri Rockets, created and directed by Russell Markert. In 1925, inspired by a UK dance troupe known as the Tiller Girls, Markert formed his own all-American version in St. Louis, Missouri, composed of girls with more diverse dance skills, longer legs, and the ability to perform higher kicks than their European counterparts. When Roxy saw them perform, he fell in love with the group's technique and showmanship, and invited them to perform as the Roxyettes at Radio City's opening night.

Samuel "Roxy" Rothafel was the mastermind behind the awe-inspiring design of Radio City Music Hall.

As legend has it, the shape of the stage was inspired by a sunset Roxy saw from the deck of a luxury ocean liner. When Radio City Music Hall was built in 1932, it was the largest theater in the world.

Russell Markert and the original Missouri Rockets, circa 1925.

The
First Night
and the First
Nighters at the
Opening of Radio
City Music Hall
in Rockefeller
Center

THE MAN RESPONSIBLE FOR RADIO CITY: JOHN D.
ROCKEFELLER JR.
on the Steps of the Grand Foyer at the Opening of the
Music Hall.
(Times Wide World Photos.)

THE STAGE AT THE OPENING PERFORMANCE OF RADIO CITY
MUSIC HALL: A SCENE FROM THE SHOW
Which Formally Opened the First Unit in Rockefeller Center, in
Which 500 Persons Took Part Before an Audience of More Than
6,000.   (Samuel H. Gottscho.)

A FAMOUS CONCERT SINGER WHO RECENTLY MADE
HIS NEW YORK DEBUT: ALFRED E. SMITH
and Mrs. Smith at the First Performance at Radio City
Music Hall.
(Times Wide World Photos.)

THE CHIEF OF STAFF AT HIS HEADQUARTERS IN
RADIO
CITY:
ROXY
at His Desk
Directing the
Army of
More Than
700 Persons
Whom He
Commanded
at the Open-
ing Perform-
ance of the
Music
Hall.

AMELIA EARHART AND JAMES MOFFETT
at the Opening of the Music Hall.
(Times Wide World Photos.)

A REPRESENTATIVE OF THE CORPORATION
WHICH OWNS THE LAND ON WHICH RADIO CITY
IS BUILT; NICHOLAS MURRAY BUTLER,
President of Columbia University, and His Daughter,
Miss Sarah Schuyler Butler.
(Times Wide World Photos.)

NELSON A. ROCKEFELLER,
Son of John D. Rockefeller Jr., With Mrs. Samuel Rothafel,
Wife of Roxy, and Mrs. T. Raymond Hood, Wife of One of the
Architects of the Music Hall.
(Times Wide World Photos.)

THE DEAN OF
BROADWAY:
DANIEL
FROHMAN
and Miss
Daisy
Humphrey.
(Times
Wide World
Photos.)

A REP-
RESENTA-
TIVE OF
THE PRIZE
RING AND
OF LITERA-
TURE: GENE
TUNNEY
in the Crowd at
the Opening of the
Music Hall.
(Times Wide World
Photos.)

INSIDE THE VAST AUDITORIUM OF THE MUSIC HALL: A VIEW ACROSS THE THEATRE
as the Crowd Assembled for the First Performance.

Radio City's opening night on December 27, 1932, featured a dizzying program of 19 separate acts, including the Flying Wallendas, Ray Bolger, Martha Graham, and the little-known Roxyettes, who made an impression on the crowd with a routine performed to the song "With a Feather in Your Cap." A veritable who's who of New York and American society turned out for the theater's debut, including William Randolph Hearst, Clark Gable, Charlie Chaplin, Amelia Earhart, Noël Coward, Irving Berlin, and of course, the Rockefellers themselves. (As many as 100,000 people vied for a spot in the theater's 6,200-seat auditorium.)

But the evening did not go smoothly. A torrential downpour and traffic jams delayed many of the evening's prominent guests, and the starting time of 8:15 p.m. was pushed to 8:45 p.m., leaving audience members restless and filled with anticipation. Additionally, the show ran long into the wee hours of the morning, forcing some critics to leave before the end in order to make their deadlines. The reviews the next day were unforgiving: one writer described the night as "a negative triumph beyond compare in the history of the entertainment industry." Worst of all, Roxy was carried from the theater on a stretcher late that same night, having suffered a heart attack.

BELOW: A program from the opening night. OPPOSITE: The *New York Times* didn't give the opening night performance at Radio City a good review, but they did photograph the large number of celebrities who attended the event.

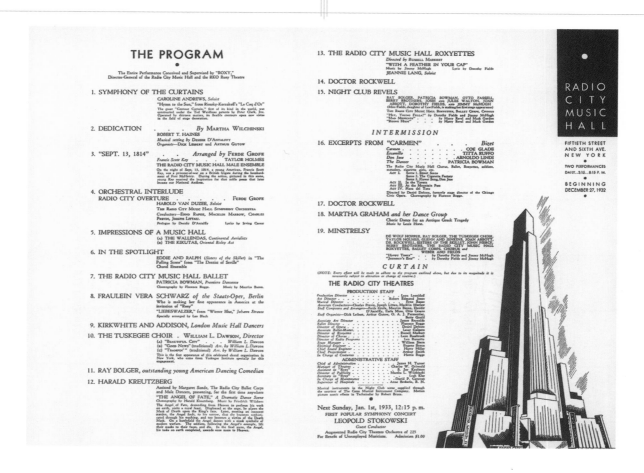

With Roxy—the guiding force of Radio City—incapacitated, and the theater already losing money, management elected to abandon the format of live revues and institute a program of movies combined with live shows. Roxy's protégé, Leon Leonidoff, stepped in to fill the shoes of his ailing mentor, and established himself as a master of theatrical spectacle in his own right.

Under the direction of Leonidoff and Markert, Radio City's program combining movie premieres and live stage shows flourished for many decades, especially during the Christmas season, with audiences returning year after year to watch the celebrated Rockettes ring in the holiday spirit with their singular dance moves.

BELOW: Markert reviews an upcoming performance with members of his troupe, circa 1950s. OPPOSITE: Leon Leonidoff with two Rockettes, 1944.

The first incarnation of the *Radio City Christmas Spectacular* occurred in 1933, with the in-house precision dance company—at this point and ever after known as the Radio City Rockettes—performing in between movie screenings as a gift from Radio City to audience members. The performance included numbers such as the "Parade of the Wooden Soldiers" and the "Living Nativity," both of which remain in the *Radio City Christmas Spectacular* to this day. For decades, the *Christmas Spectacular* also brought audiences the talents of the Corps de Ballet and the 60-member Radio City Music Hall Glee Club, as well as novelty acts such as gymnasts, dancing dogs and bears, and comedians.

The first *Radio City Christmas Spectacular* included the breathtaking Renaissance-inspired "Living Nativity."

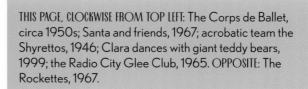

During the first 40 years of its history, Radio City Music Hall was a favorite place for moviemakers to premiere their films. The first film to be screened was the Frank Capra movie *The Bitter Tea of General Yen*. It premiered just two weeks after the theater's opening gala in 1933. Since then, more than 700 movies have opened at the Music Hall, including the original *King Kong*, *Breakfast at Tiffany's*, and *To Kill a Mockingbird*, starring former Radio City usher Gregory Peck.

The 6,000-seat auditorium was a magnificent place to watch a movie. From the Grand Foyer and the elegant lounges to the uniformed ushers that escorted patrons to their seats, not a single detail was overlooked. The popularity of the theater thrived through the 1940s, '50s, and '60s—movies that premiered at Radio City Music Hall almost always had successful runs at theaters across the country.

But by the late 1970s, New York City was in the grip of an economic crisis, and Radio City Music Hall found it increasingly difficult to fill its seats with movie audiences. In 1978, the theater announced that its final performance would take place on April 12 of that year. On the evening of that last performance, Radio City was saved from the wrecking ball, having been declared a New York City landmark.

In an effort to make the theater more economically viable, Radio City management decided to stop showing movies and use the theater as a venue for live performances—everything from concerts to award shows—similar to Roxy's original vision. The *Radio City Christmas Spectacular* grew to a 90-minute seasonal extravaganza.

BELOW: More than 22 films starring Cary Grant premiered at Radio City Music Hall, giving him plenty of opportunities to pose with the Radio City Rockettes, circa 1950s. OPPOSITE: The Radio City Corps of Ushers prepare for the evening show, circa 1950s.

The late 1990s brought more changes to Radio City Music Hall, this time in the form of a new owner. In 1997, Cablevision signed a 25-year lease on the building, and the company embarked on an eight-month, $70 million restoration project, which returned the Music Hall to its original 1932 splendor.

In 1998, Radio City Music Hall underwent an extensive renovation, restoring the grand theater to its earlier glory.

The *Christmas Spectacular* has seen countless changes over the years, but no matter what film was screened, which acts took to the stage, or what dazzling costumes the Rockettes donned, it has never failed to delight audiences with its splendor and true embodiment of the holiday spirit.

Nearly eight decades after Radio City Music Hall first opened its doors, it remains one of the greatest theaters on earth and more than 68 million people have been thrilled by the *Radio City Christmas Spectacular*, one of America's most treasured shows.

The stunning finale to the 1947 *Christmas Spectacular* included the entire company onstage.

CHAPTER TWO

PLANNING A SPECTACULAR

NOT EVERY SHOW CAN BE CALLED A "SPECTACULAR," but Radio City's Christmas production earns the title in every respect. For each performer who crosses the Music Hall's stage, there is someone behind the scenes who helps make the production possible—from the producers and director who nurture the show in its earliest form to the stage managers who ensure it runs without a hitch, to the designers who build the larger-than-life sets and create the vibrant collection of costumes, to the choreographers who are responsible for the complex dance routines. This crew of artists and artisans works all year long to present the most popular live holiday show in the world.

The Rockettes dance in Times Square, circa 1949. The set designer did a clever job rewriting the advertisements and including a sign pointing toward Radio City.

BEHIND THE SCENES

Since 1933, Radio City has brought the *Christmas Spectacular* to its devoted audience each season without fail. The show requires as much artistry and choreography backstage as it does onstage. Currently, the production staff of each show includes 23 carpenters, 20 electricians, 15 prop people, 7 sound technicians, 28 wardrobe staff members, 2 projectionists, 8 animal handlers, and a 40-member orchestra.

Rockettes backstage, 1954.

Roxy was the mastermind behind many of the theater's early technological wonders, and today's producers continue to incorporate the latest and greatest technology into the production. In recent years, they have added 3-D animation and utilized the theater's LED screen, which is the largest free-hanging screen in the world.

When the show's producers began planning the 75th celebration of the *Christmas Spectacular* they worked hard to maintain the nostalgic elements while updating the show. They wanted to include the moments that people have come to love and want to see every year, but at the same time, look forward and bring the show into the 21st century, with all of the new technological abilities that didn't exist years ago. The end production was the perfect mix of new and old with the "Parade of the Wooden Soldiers" along side a 3-D sleigh ride with Santa.

The result of nearly a year of planning is a 90-minute extravaganza that runs smoothly onstage despite the organized chaos backstage. That's thanks in part to a very calm and focused group of stage managers who oversee the entire production.

During the performance, as the behind-the-scenes controlled mayhem swirls around, the production stage manager "calls" the show from a tiny desk in the wings, with just enough room for a book of cues and a light. Four other stage managers, stationed around the backstage area and equipped with radio headsets and walkie-talkies, manage the run of the show. Do things ever go wrong? Of course. But the Radio City crew—considered one of the best in the business—has a very long list of "what ifs" and is prepared to react within seconds to solve any problem. Usually, the audience is never even aware that something has gone awry.

And when everything works (which is 99 percent of the time), it works amazingly well. As the Rockettes are spinning and dancing on a replica of a double-decker bus, just six feet away a section of the stage is 14 feet below, being prepped with an ice rink and skaters in just one minute and ten seconds.

There is one particular scene change that is especially challenging for production stage manager Kathy Hoovler: the transition from a number with dozens of Rockettes dancing as Santa Clauses to the rag doll number in Santa's workshop. "I have scaffolding that's 27 feet tall that has to go down an elevator 27 feet into the basement. I have scenery that moves automatically. Once it's set, I have to place Santa's house. The Rockettes have to change from their Santa costumes into rag doll costumes, and then go down two flights to load onto the big shelf unit. Meanwhile, I have two small kids and a Santa Claus flying in a snowstorm. Plus, I'm moving an orchestra out of the orchestra pit so it doesn't get snowed on. All of this has to be accomplished in two minutes and 20 seconds. It takes every stage manager, every human being that is working back there to make it happen!"

Radio City management plans the upcoming *Christmas Spectacular*, circa 1960s. From left: Charles Hacker, vice president; Russell V. Downing, president; James Stewart Morcom, set designer; Leon Leonidoff, senior producer; Russell Markert, producer and director of the Rockettes.

Bear costumes line the wall and Santa's sleigh waits in the wings, backstage at Radio City Music Hall, 2004.

SET DESIGN AND CONSTRUCTION

An integral part of the *Christmas Spectacular* is the onstage spectacle that surrounds the production's 160-plus performers. The massive set pieces have included towering Christmas trees, a three-story cabinet in Santa's workshop, a full-size circus ring, and enormous Wedgwood plates with the Rockettes as decorative details.

A Rockette poses before the stage rendering of the 1972 Christmas production, which was inspired by Hallmark greeting cards.

Of course, the sets are created with the goal of astounding the audience with their grand scale, but the sheer size of the stage itself dictates that whatever is placed on it must match its grandeur in order to have an impact.

Designed by theatrical engineer Peter Clark, the great stage is 144 feet wide (almost an entire city block) and 66 feet deep. A brilliantly conceived hydraulics system powers three sections of the stage and a central turntable, all of which can be raised to 13 feet above the stage or lowered to a subbasement 27 feet below. (The mechanical design was so revolutionary at the time the theater was built that the U.S. Navy studied it to devise a similar elevator system for its aircraft carriers.) The sculptured curtain, which weighs 1,800 pounds, is powered by 13 individual motors.

BELOW: The state-of-art hydraulic system that powers the three sections of the stage. OPPOSITE: Stagehands help raise the curtain, which weighs 1,800 pounds.

The process of creating new set pieces that can go head to head with the scale of the Radio City stage begins almost as soon as the curtain falls on a season's final performance. In early January, the show's director and lead set designer begin reviewing the script for the upcoming year, adjusting and revising the vision for several weeks. Initial designs take the form of pencil and thumbnail sketches, which then evolve into a visual description of the show as a storyboard. Computer renderings of the designs are then made, followed by a white paper model, and finally a color model. Then it's time to build.

In shops as far away as Los Angeles and Chicago, and as near as the borough of Brooklyn, the sets are built from materials such as steel, plywood, canvas, and aluminum. Meanwhile, sets being reused from the previous year are inspected for any wear and tear when they come out of storage, then spruced up by painters and other artisans for the coming season.

THIS PAGE: No trimmings were forgotten, from garlands to a giant Christmas card, on the 1961 set. OPPOSITE, CLOCKWISE FROM TOP LEFT: The 1946 set was inspired by Christmas traditions from around the world; the focus was on three giant aluminum Christmas trees in 1973; the Rockettes danced around a carousel in 1934; a small-town winter wonderland was erected circa 1975; Christmas trees filled the stage in 1955.

Ballet

#401

use old trees (too little, I think) we should
make 2 new trees — bring them in from each
side with *mirror balls* on them — let girls go
up into trees (2 levels) & then swing mirrors —

Rockettes pop out of larger-than-life stockings—an extraordinary gift from Santa. INSET: The original sketch for the 1950 set.

The *Christmas Spectacular*'s scenic backdrops measure an astounding 45 feet high and 95 feet wide, while the custom-made double-decker bus, featured in the "New York at Christmas" scene in 2007, is 34 feet long and weighs seven tons. (To give a sense of just how big the stage is, many stages in New York City's theater district have 32-foot-wide performance spaces, which wouldn't even fit the double-decker bus.)

Just a little more than a week before the *Christmas Spectacular* opens, the Radio City crew installs all of the show's set pieces at the theater. During the 90-minute run of the show, most of the set pieces are stored above the stage, using 20 chain hoists and 65,000 pounds of counterweight. Other elements are housed in the building's subbasement below the stage. In the off-season, the sets are stored in warehouses outside New York City, awaiting an exciting new season of the *Radio City Christmas Spectacular*.

BELOW: The backdrop for the 1958 production was a beautiful illustration of a department store window. OPPOSITE, CLOCKWISE FROM TOP LEFT: The sketch of the big top scenery for "Stars and Spangles" and the final product, which was the perfect backdrop for the circus that took place onstage, 1944; the set designers created a blizzard onstage in 1947; New York City's Time Square came to life in 2007.

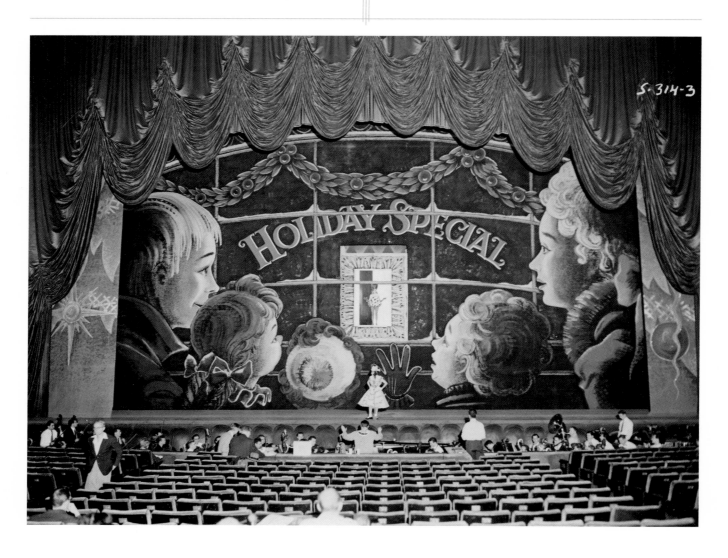

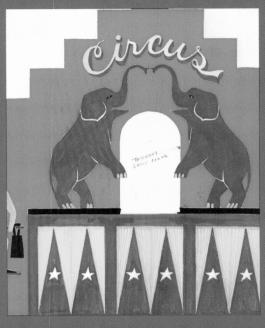

A team of seamstresses creates costumes for the Rockettes, circa 1960s.

DESIGNING THE SHOW'S COSTUMES

Rag dolls. Dancing acorns. Reindeer with electrified antlers. And of course, iconic and crisp wooden soldiers sporting perfectly pressed pants. These are just a few of the looks the Rockettes have donned in the *Radio City Christmas Spectacular* over the decades. Year after year, audiences fill Radio City Music Hall during the holidays to see those famous eye-high kicks—but they also come to see the costumes, which are nothing short of dazzling.

Rockette
Astronauts

Creators of the Rockettes' costumes throughout the show's history include Vincente Minnelli (whose 1933 design for the "Parade of the Wooden Soldiers" costume, inspired by a porcelain doll, remains unchanged to this day), Erté (who also designed costumes for the *Ziegfeld Follies*), and legendary fashion designer Bob Mackie. Additionally, famed Broadway designers James Morcom, John William Keck, Marco Montedoro, and Frank Spencer have outfitted the company for the holiday season.

The Rockettes' costumes have changed with the times. In 1965, "Destination Moon" landed the ladies in astronaut suits; a 1972 production, entitled "Greetings" and inspired by Hallmark cards, dressed the line as Salvation Army "Femail Carriers;" and the 1999 "White Christmas in New York" number cast the troupe as mannequins dressed in platinum wigs and mirrors. Perhaps not surprisingly, hemlines have progressively inched up since the 1930s.

OPPOSITE: A sketch for the astronaut-inspired costumes for the scene "Destination Moon," 1965. THIS PAGE, TOP: A Rockette demonstrates to Markert the flexibility of the costume; BOTTOM: The final ethereal designs onstage.

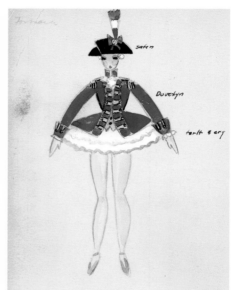

THIS PAGE, CLOCKWISE FROM TOP LEFT: Corps de Ballet colonial toy soldier costume and its corresponding sketch, 1936; the Rockettes' poodle costume created for the scene "Puttin' on the Dog," 1948; the zebra costume sketch from the scene "Jungle Belles," 1956. OPPOSITE: Two Rockettes model the finished design, 1956.

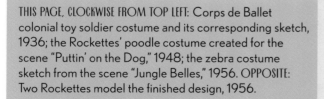

The process of creating a new Rockette costume takes many months, and begins with a list of adjectives provided to the costume designer by the show's director and choreographer. When costume designer Frank Krenz set about to design costumes for the 2007 number "Let Christmas Shine," he was inspired in part by the director's desire to see something that was "modern deco."

Next, numerous sketches are drawn, reviewed, and refined. A single handmade version of a preliminary design is then executed on a mannequin, and after some fine-tuning, yet another sample garment is created. Upon final approval, the design is mass-produced.

As Krenz sees it, a successful Rockette costume celebrates the troupe's heritage, includes both an all-American girl element as well as a bit of sex appeal, and honors the group's formidable athleticism.

Yet another change in the Rockettes' costumes is a turn to the more durable. With the routines becoming more physically demanding, the outfits have responded in kind. Gone is the more delicate chiffon and beaded detailing; Rockettes' costumes now fit close to the body and feature sturdy shiny trim to accommodate their increasingly athletic numbers.

But the elements of the *Christmas Spectacular* costumes go far beyond sparkling dresses or simple suits. The Rockettes alone go through 1,400 pairs of pantyhose and 30,000 red dots—worn on their cheeks for the "Parade of the Wooden Soldiers" and "Rag Doll" numbers—during the show's eight-week seasonal run. The entire cast of 160 performers wear more than 1,200 pairs of shoes during the *Christmas Spectacular*. All in all, more than 1,300 costumes cross the stage over the course of 90 magical minutes. (And at least 350 loads of laundry are done each week.)

The task of maintaining every element of every costume—which often includes tights, gloves, earrings, hats, and more—and making sure they are all in the right place at the right time, falls to the wardrobe supervisor, who also orchestrates costume changes during the show.

"It may look overwhelming to have five racks of costumes rolling onto the wings with the Rockettes changing out of their wooden soldier costumes and into their 'Christmas in New York' costumes in less than two minutes," says wardrobe supervisor Barbara Van Zandt, "but it's really very well organized."

OPPOSITE, CLOCKWISE FROM TOP LEFT: Mother Goose costume from the ballet "Old King Cole," 1939; Two of the three kings from the "Living Nativity," 1935; grasshopper, 1932; drummer from the ballet "Coppelia," 1933; a Corps de Ballet peasant costume, 1933; a Rockette mouse costume from "Old King Cole," 1939; glee club costumes for the "Living Nativity," 1936; a Corps de Ballet angel costume, 1934; a Rockette snowman costume, 1935.

The secret to executing these lighting-speed changes offstage is an experienced crew of 25 dressers, and as Van Zandt puts it "well-trained Rockettes," who learn very quickly how to unzip the woman in front of them as they exit the stage, and throw costume pieces into laundry baskets if they aren't sure where an item should go. "You can't come offstage and just kick off your shoes," Van Zandt says. "I can't tell you how many times we've been on the floor trying to find something. The laundry basket is key. I must have four or five hundred of them."

The costume changes happen in every square inch available backstage. Quick change rooms measuring 12-feet by 15-feet located off both stage right and left will be filled with as many as 18 Rockettes and five dressers in between numbers. Even then, some of the cast make costume changes in hallways. "Wherever you find a little spot, generally somebody's going to be changing their clothes there," says Van Zandt.

To be sure, the costumes of the *Radio City Christmas Spectacular* will continue to evolve, but no matter what the cast of the seasonal show is wearing, there are three things audiences are guaranteed: sparkle of the season, plenty of surprises, and yes, those wooden soldiers and their pressed pants.

THIS PAGE: Last minute touches to a costume, 2005. OPPOSITE: Rockettes costume sketch, 1977.

The Rockettes
Christmas 1977
Peter Gennaro

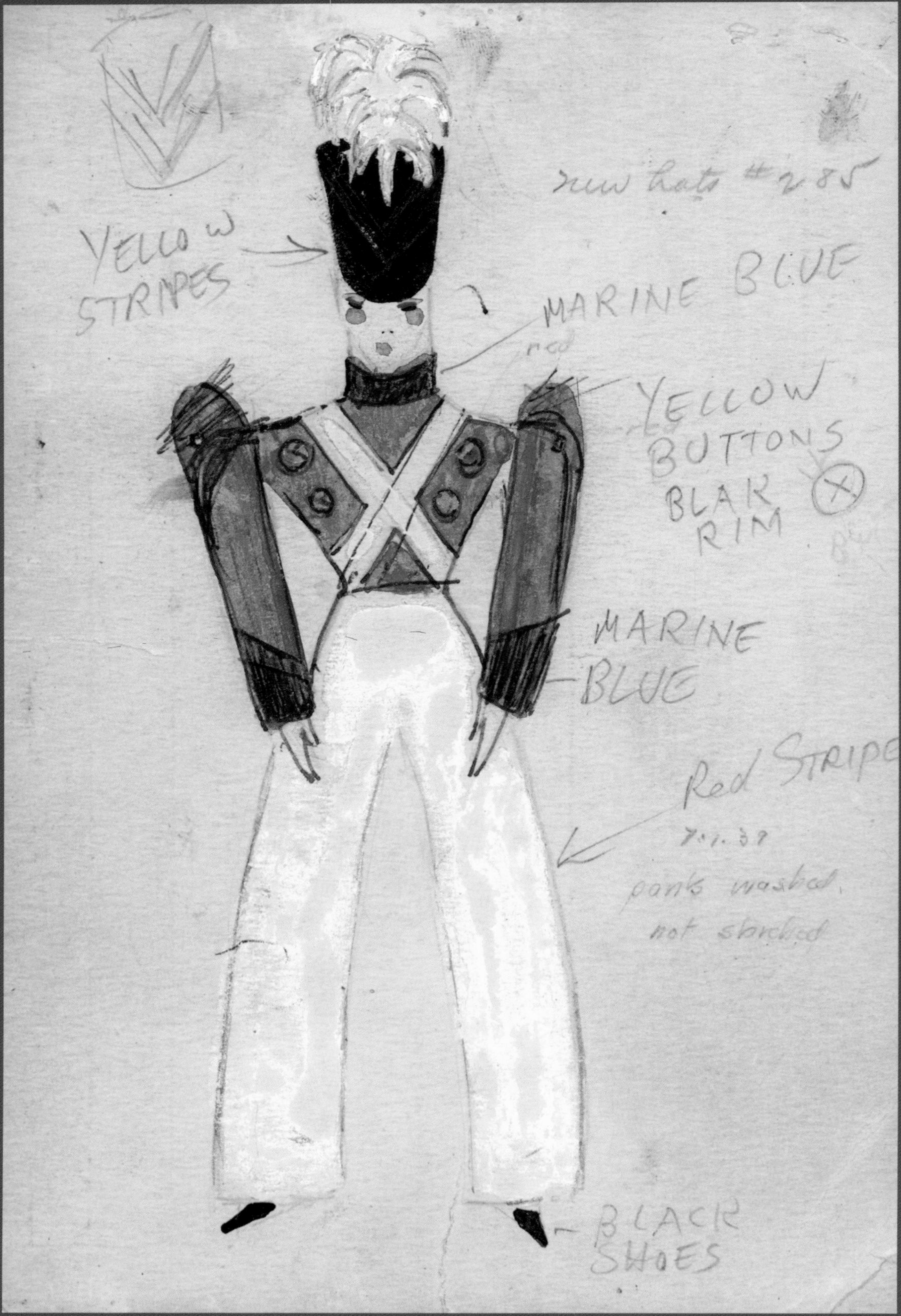

OPPOSITE: Vincente Minnelli designed the wooden soldier costume for the first Christmas show in 1933.
THIS PAGE: A similar costume is still being worn today.

CHOREOGRAPHING THE ROCKETTES

Imagine 36 women—and 72 legs—moving in perfect harmony. It's the hallmark of the Radio City Rockettes and something they seem to do effortlessly show after show. But just how, exactly, do they do it?

Russell Markert, who founded the Rockettes in 1925 (initially known at the Missouri Rockets), continued to choreograph the troupe's routines until 1971, when he retired from the Music Hall at age 72. He is the creator of the famed "Parade of the Wooden Soldiers" routine and inspired many dances that are still performed today.

Those famous legs.

The numbers performed throughout the *Christmas Spectacular* begin to take shape many months ahead of opening night, and far away from the dance studio and stage. They are first born as a concept in the director's mind: a patriotic sequence that includes tap dancing, a routine that fills the stage with dozens of identical Santas, a celebration of the circus with the women dressed as wild animals.

CLOCKWISE FROM TOP LEFT: As dancing Santas, 1999; stunning in red and white, 1973; performing their famous high kick in "Jungle Belles," 1956; in patriotic form, 1940.

Once the overall look and feel of the number is determined, the director meets with the show's dance arranger, who helps build the music to the dance sequences. The formations of each dance will often be sketched out on graph paper at this point in the process to ensure that trademark precision and make certain there is enough space for each Rockette on the stage.

Next, as few as two dancers will work with the director and the dance arranger to test run the formations and work out any kinks. (For example, a few more bars of music may be needed to get the Rockettes from one end of the stage to the other.) The routine is then tested by a larger group of 12 Rockettes before it is practiced and performed by the full line.

The Rockettes rehearse for the show six days a week for four weeks in the studio. The first task is simply learning the steps of each routine. But the dancers must then refine their movements to make sure they are in exactly the right place with every step they take and also be certain that every pinkie finger, elbow, and toe are positioned precisely the same way. Constant repetition is a huge part of the process. Two weeks before the opening night, the group takes to the stage to rehearse even more, first with lighting and stage cues, and finally, in costume.

Russell Markert and the Rockettes practice the eye-high kick line that made the precision dance company world-famous, 1946.

THIS PAGE, CLOCKWISE FROM TOP LEFT: Practicing line kicks, circa 1950s; rehearsing the "Parade of the Wooden Soliders," 2003; trying out the steps for "12 Days Of Christmas," 2006. OPPOSITE: Showing off the perfect high kick, 1955.

Thankfully, the dancers do have some help in re-creating their precision routines day in and day out. The massive Music Hall stage is marked with solid, dotted, and colored guidelines for the dancers to use as reference points, as well as numbers along the front edge of the stage and detailed charts mapping out every sequence in a routine. Additionally, the troupe uses techniques such as "guiding off" (using peripheral vision to make sure one is in line correctly), "splitting a number" (lining up perfectly with a number downstage), and determining a single point to focus on, such as the theater's second mezzanine, so that every dancer is looking in the same direction during a sequence such as a kick line.

"It certainly has become more difficult to be a Rockette," says Linda Haberman, the show's director and the mastermind of the Rockettes' routines. "And not just in terms of athleticism and stamina, which it has, but style-wise and artistically. I think much more is demanded of the Rockettes now. It's not enough to put a smile on your face and just dance around. They just keep getting better—as dancers, as actors, as a group."

The Rockettes grace the grand stage at Radio City Music Hall, with the Manhattan skyline as a backdrop, circa 1990s.

ANIMALS BACKSTAGE

The *Christmas Spectacular* would not be complete without the participation of the four-legged members of the cast, which has included camels, sheep, donkeys, a horse, and even a reindeer. In the early days of the show, when novelty acts were included, Radio City played hosts to bears, chimps, and even an elephant or two.

An animal handler at Radio City Music Hall takes a reindeer from the *Christmas Spectacular* on a walk through the streets surrounding Rockefeller Center during a blizzard, 1996. INSET: The Rockettes pose backstage with an even bigger star, Tanya the Elephant, 1969.

During the course of the show's run, the animals live at the Music Hall in hay-filled stalls, with their handlers sleeping in a small cabin nearby. The menagerie consumes 450 bottles of water, 340 bales of hay, and 560 loaves of seven-grain bread over the show's eight-week run, and is exercised daily with early-morning and late-night strolls on the streets outside Radio City—an occurrence that has surprised more than a few New York night owls and Midtown commuters.

THIS PAGE, TOP: A Rockette holds a chimp from the Christmas show's novelty acts, circa 1950s; BOTTOM: The "Living Nativity" camels take a walk through Rockefeller Center, 2002. OPPOSITE: The Rockettes with a reindeer from the "Living Nativity," circa 2000s.

CHAPTER THREE

THE SHOW

THE ENTERTAINMENT AT RADIO CITY MUSIC HALL has changed over the theater's storied history, but there is one show that returns to the stage each year without fail: the *Radio City Christmas Spectacular*. With sellout performances through the holiday season, this intrinsically New York holiday tradition officially began in 1933, nearly one year after the Hall's notorious opening night. Of course, Santa Claus and the Rockettes have always played key roles in the show, but many other acts have been a part of the *Christmas Spectacular*. The Music Hall's Corps de Ballet were an essential part of the production for many years, as was the Glee Club. And a variety of novelty acts have also taken the stage—from acrobats to dancing monkeys—entertaining and surprising the holiday crowds over the decades.

The 1952 *Christmas Spectacular* finale, "Parade of the Holidays."

The inaugural show on December 21, 1933, entitled *Coppelia*, featured the adaptation of a popular ballet of the same name, the screening of the film *Flying Down to Rio*, scenery designed by art director Vincente Minnelli (the Academy Award–winning director, and father to Liza, worked for Radio City for just three years), and the Rockettes, who performed such beloved numbers as the "Parade of the Wooden Soldiers" and the "Living Nativity."

BELOW: A program from the first *Christmas Spectacular.*
OPPOSITE: The Rockettes performed "On a Christmas Tree" dressed as baby dolls, 1933.

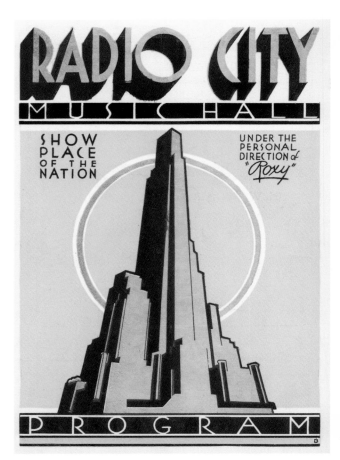

THE RADIO CITY NOVELTY ACTS

From its inception in the 1930s until the late '70s, the *Radio City Christmas Spectacular* not only promised audiences the appearance of the Hall's star dance company, the Rockettes; the live stage review also featured performances by wild and wonderful novelty acts. Everything from horses, to dogs, to acrobats took to the stage throughout the show's history.

Thrilling acrobatics, 1951.

The *Christmas Spectacular* in 1940 featured Bill Baird's Marionettes; 1948's "Star Spangled" circus extravaganza included a performance by Pallenberg's Bears; and in 1952 Al Jansley's French poodles delighted the crowd with "Dog Antics." The world-famous Lippizaner Horses graced the stage in 1944, the year the Music Hall screened *National Velvet*. "Good Ship Holiday" in 1946 hosted the acrobatic group the Shyrettos (who performed with Ringling Bros. and Barnum & Bailey circus) and their "Fun on Wheels" routine, and 1961's "Holiday Tidings" welcomed back the Martha Graham Dancers and the Flying Wallendas, both of whom performed at Radio City's 1932 opening night. Radio City audiences never quite knew what whimsical act they'd be treated to next, but they were guaranteed it would feature the best variety talent in the world.

THIS PAGE: Pallenberg's famous bears perform "Playmates," 1948. OPPOSITE, CLOCKWISE FROM TOP LEFT: 1944's screening of *National Velvet* included Gautier's Steeple Chase; Van Leer's Eight Champing Champions took the stage in 1941; poodles showed off their dancing skills in 1943.

THIS PAGE: Lilly Yokoi shows off her cycling skills, 1961.
OPPOSITE, CLOCKWISE FROM TOP: The Rogge Sisters, 1965;
Clauson's World Famous Act "Goldilocks and the Bears,"
1954; the Mascott Sisters, 1957.

THE MUSIC HALL GLEE CLUB

The Music Hall Glee Club was an important part of the *Radio City Christmas Spectacular* during the early years of the show. The 60-member group performed original song-and-dance numbers for a captive audience. Whether it was the "Silly Symphony," with Glee Club members in clown costumes or "Ski Valley Express," which transported the audience to a winter wonderland, the group was always entertaining.

Erno Rapee, one of America's most prolific symphonic conductors, created original music for the group during his tenure as musical director and head conductor of Radio City Music Hall, from 1932 until his death in 1945.

"Silly Symphony," 1948.

The Music Hall Glee Club channels Elvis Presley with their lively number "Jingle Jangle," 1956.

THE MUSIC HALL CORPS DE BALLET

One of Roxy's visions for Radio City Music Hall was a permanent in-house ballet company known as the Corps de Ballet. His dedication to this idea was revolutionary at the time. In 1932, ballet was largely unknown by general American audiences. The Corps de Ballet danced along with the Rockettes at every Christmas performance, and the company included such ballet luminaries as Patricia Bowman and Melissa Hayden. Corps de Ballet numbers over the years included "Snowflakes," "Here Come the Clowns," "Jolly Holly," and "With Trumpet and Drum." The company was an ongoing topic of financial debate among Music Hall management and was finally disbanded in 1974, but the audience favorites, the Radio City Rockettes, continued to be an integral part of the *Christmas Spectacular*.

The Music Hall Corps de Ballet pose as a Christmas tree, 1940.

"The Gilded Cage," 1944, was choreographed by Florence Rogge, who served as the ballet mistress and chief choreographer for the company's first 20 years.

THIS PAGE: The Corps de Ballet perform "Yuletidings," 1949. OPPOSITE, TOP: The Alpine-inspired number "Skiing Under Northern Skies," 1946; BOTTOM: Dancing in a picturesque small town, 1966.

Continuing the tradition of ballet at Radio City Music Hall, the *Christmas Spectacular* includes a tribute to the classic holiday ballet *The Nutcracker*. Under a giant glittering Christmas tree, and to the tune of Tchaikovsky's familiar classical composition, a young girl named Clara dances with cuddly bears who come to life. The dance features baby bears, panda bears, Russian Cossack bears, and tutu-clad bears. The Radio City interpretation of this favorite holiday ballet brings to life a childhood fantasy, and is a favorite of young audience members.

THIS PAGE, TOP: Clara is lifted gracefully into the air by a giant teddy bear, 1999; BOTTOM: Teddy bears dressed as ballerinas perform, 1999. OPPOSITE: A dream come true—dancing with life-size teddy bears, 2007.

THE ROCKETTES

The Radio City Rockettes are one of the most celebrated, glamorous, and well-known precision dance companies in the world. This troupe of 36 eye-high kicking dancers is an icon of New York City and an intrinsic part of the holiday season for millions of people.

Since the group's inception in 1925, the standard for the Rockettes has been nothing short of excellence. The group's routines, drawing on a variety of dance skills, have only increased in complexity and showmanship throughout the *Christmas Spectacular*'s history. Amazingly, this one-of-a-kind troupe just keeps getting better and better, a feat no doubt due to the fact that the Rockettes are the hardest working dancers in show business.

The 1937 *Christmas Spectacular* had the Rockettes dressed as dolls and perched high in Santa's toy closet.

In the 1930s and '40s, the Rockettes lived at the Music Hall, performing at night and rehearsing during the day. (It was not unusual for the company to practice the routine for an upcoming show late at night after an evening's final screening.) The 1932 Rockettes made $48 a week working 16-hour days, seven days a week. Facilities for the women included dorms, a nurse's office, a cafeteria, and a recreation space on the roof of the building. (The corps of regimented male ushers at the hall also maintained their own suite of bunks onsite.)

Today's Rockettes lead very different lives from their 1930s and '40s counterparts. Many of them are, of course, professional dancers—several of whom perform on Broadway when they are not gracing the Radio City stage—but the current company also includes lawyers, mothers, entrepreneurs, students, Pilates instructors, and actresses. Over the years, the women who have proudly called themselves Radio City Rockettes have not only danced the same steps but share a unique experience as part of an enduring legacy.

THIS PAGE: During the busy holiday season, the Rockettes spend much of their time at Radio City Music Hall, so they add some of their own holiday touches backstage, circa 1970s. OPPOSITE: The Rockettes have lunch backstage before a performance, circa 1950s.

Russell Markert, the founder and director of the Rockettes (originally known as the Missouri Rockets), had a specific list of requirements he considered when choosing the women for his troupe. Besides the ability to kick to eye level, prospective dancers had to have a pretty (though not necessarily beautiful) face, a good figure, a proficiency in tap, jazz, and ballet, and the right personality—one that could project from a stage but not hog the spotlight. Uniformity—and the ability to perform as part of a single, synchronized unit—was key to the success of the troupe.

The qualities that make an ideal Rockette have changed very little over the years. The women must be between 5' 6" and 5' 10", be athletically fit, and have that special element of "shine." Hopefuls who audition are asked to learn a dance routine on the spot and run through it once without music, and then once with music. After that, they take to the floor to be judged by the troupe's choreographers and director. Those lucky enough to make it through the first round return the next day for yet more scrutiny. Auditions for the company frequently attract hundreds of aspiring Rockettes, with as few as two dancers making the final cut.

THIS PAGE: Linda Haberman leads potential Rockettes through the precision dance moves, 2007. OPPOSITE: Hundreds of aspiring dancers line up outside Radio City before a Rockette audition.

THIS PAGE, CLOCKWISE FROM TOP: "Dance of the Snowflakes," 1947; in Christmas tree costumes, 1937; as mannequins in "White Christmas in New York," 1999. OPPOSITE: The Rockettes perform as rag dolls perched high in Santa's toy cabinet, 2007.

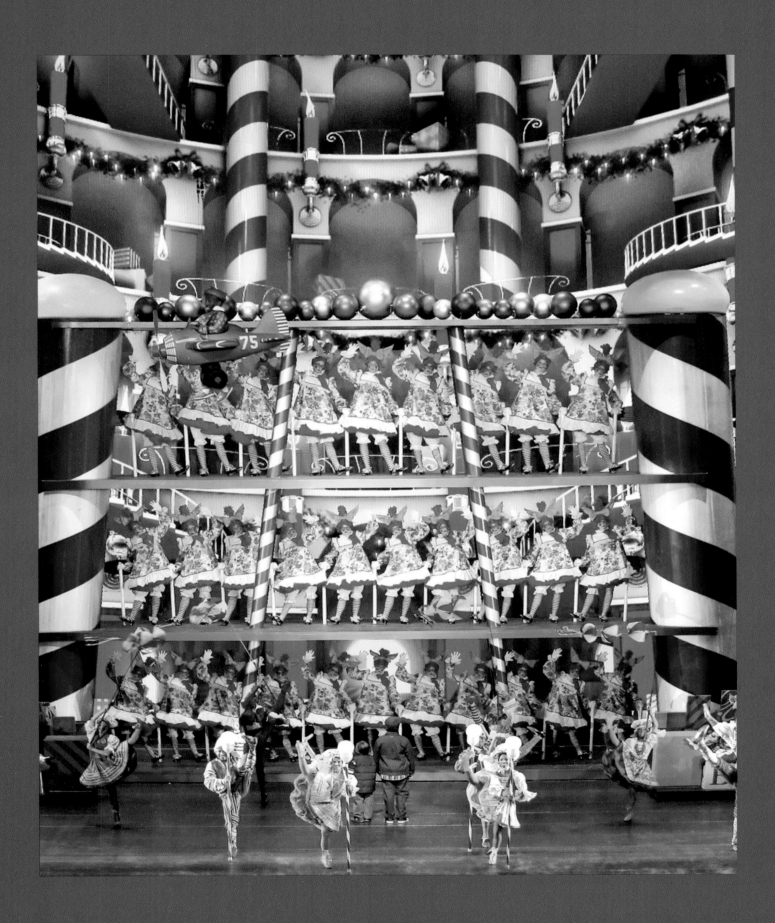

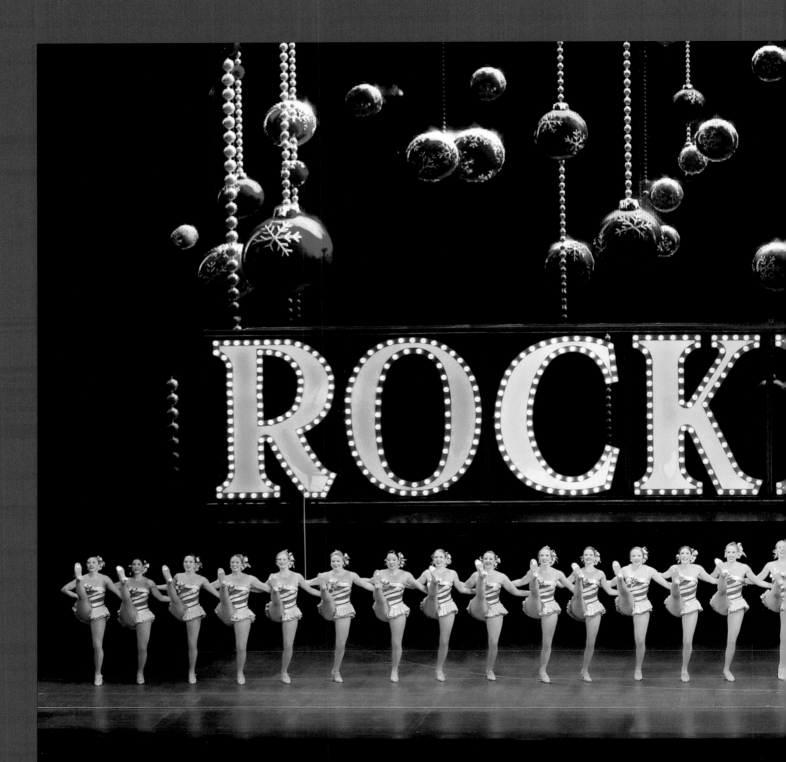

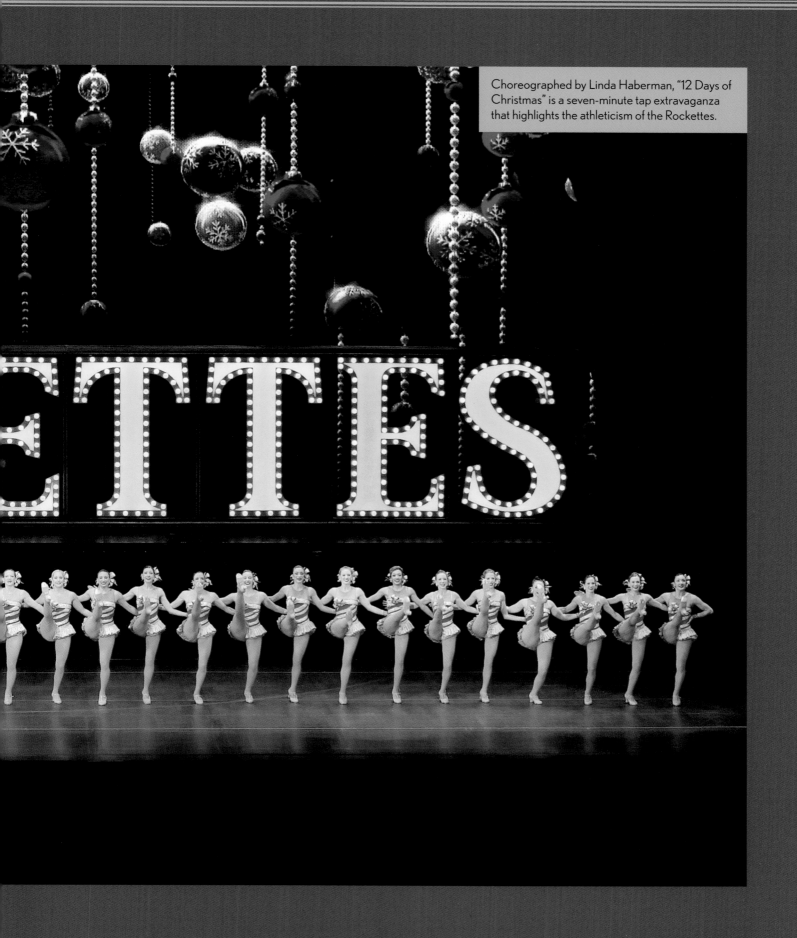

Choreographed by Linda Haberman, "12 Days of Christmas" is a seven-minute tap extravaganza that highlights the athleticism of the Rockettes.

Everyone knows and loves the Rockettes' signature precision move: those perfectly timed, stunning eye-high kicks. In a five-show day, each Rockette will perform as many as 1,500 kicks. Key to the company's uniformity onstage is the placement of the tallest women in the middle of the line and the shortest ones at each end; the result is an optical illusion that makes the dancers appear as if they are all the same height.

The Rockettes are trained in jazz, tap, and ballet, and their routines incorporate the classic ballet lines of George Balanchine, the showy jazz hands of Bob Fosse, and the Rockettes' own signature high-energy aerobic moves. The physical demands of the dances have increased over the years, from the rambunctious "Rag Dolls" sequence at Santa's workshop to the seven-minute tap marathon of "12 Days of Christmas." With the almost nonstop schedule of the *Christmas Spectacular*, it's not uncommon for Rockettes to spend whatever downtime they have between shows submerging their tired feet and legs in giant tubs of water. The Rockettes are much more than dancers—they are athletes.

Although thrilling and rewarding, it has never been easy to be a Rockette—they just make it look that way with their tireless glamour and poise.

The Radio City Rockettes board a double-decker bus for a tour of Manhattan, taking the audience along for a ride, 2007.

MUSIC HALL
Music Hall
RADIO CITY
75TH YEAR CELEBRATION
GRAY LINE
New York Sightseeing
GRAY LINE

THE PARADE OF THE WOODEN SOLDIERS

No *Radio City Christmas Spectacular* would be complete without the "Parade of the Wooden Soldiers." The routine, featuring the Rockettes in bright red jackets, three-foot high hats, and crisply starched pants, has amazed audiences since the show's debut in 1933. Both the choreography by the group's founder, Russell Markert, and the striking costumes designed by Vincente Minnelli remain virtually unchanged to this day. This stunning display of precision and seemingly effortless grace has become the Rockettes' signature number and is a highly anticipated event at every *Christmas Spectacular* performance.

"Parade of the Wooden Soliders," 1999.

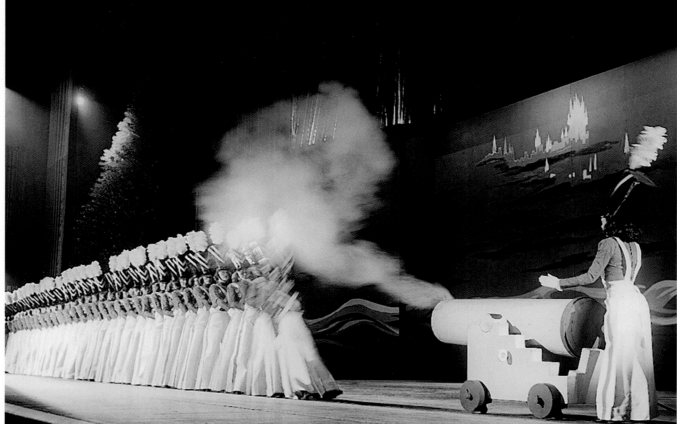

THIS PAGE: The fall, 1999. OPPOSITE, TOP: Santa sets up the cannon, 1972; BOTTOM: The soldiers are knocked over in a puff of smoke, circa 1940s.

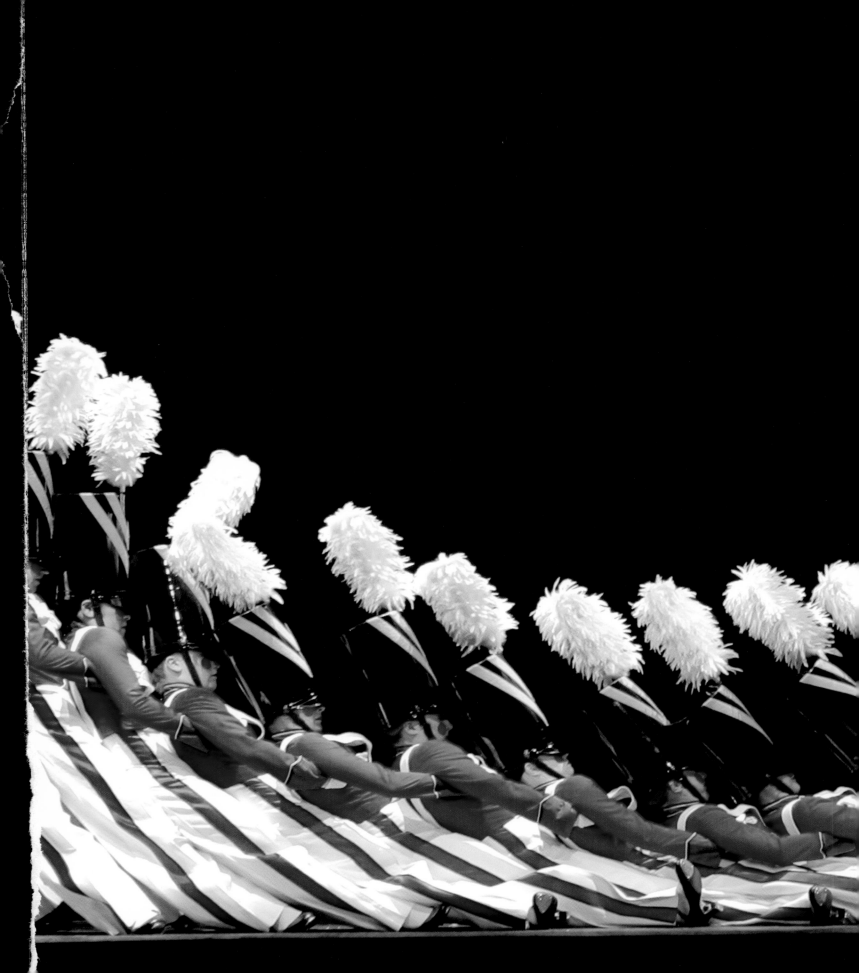

Russell Markert's clever choreography makes "Parade of the Wooden Soliders" as entertaining today as it was when it first debuted in 1933. THIS PAGE: The soliders prepare to be felled, 1937. GATEFOLD: The Wooden Soldiers, 2006.

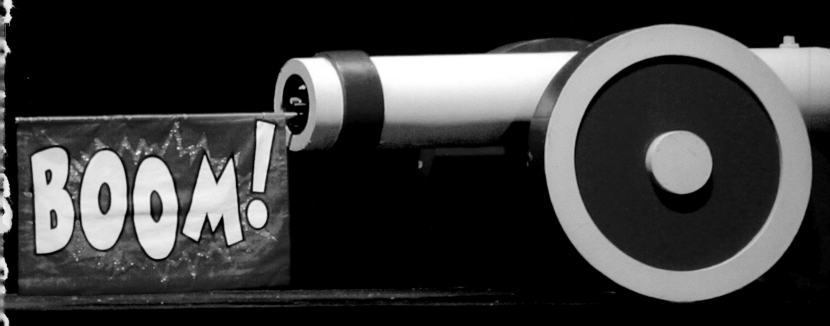

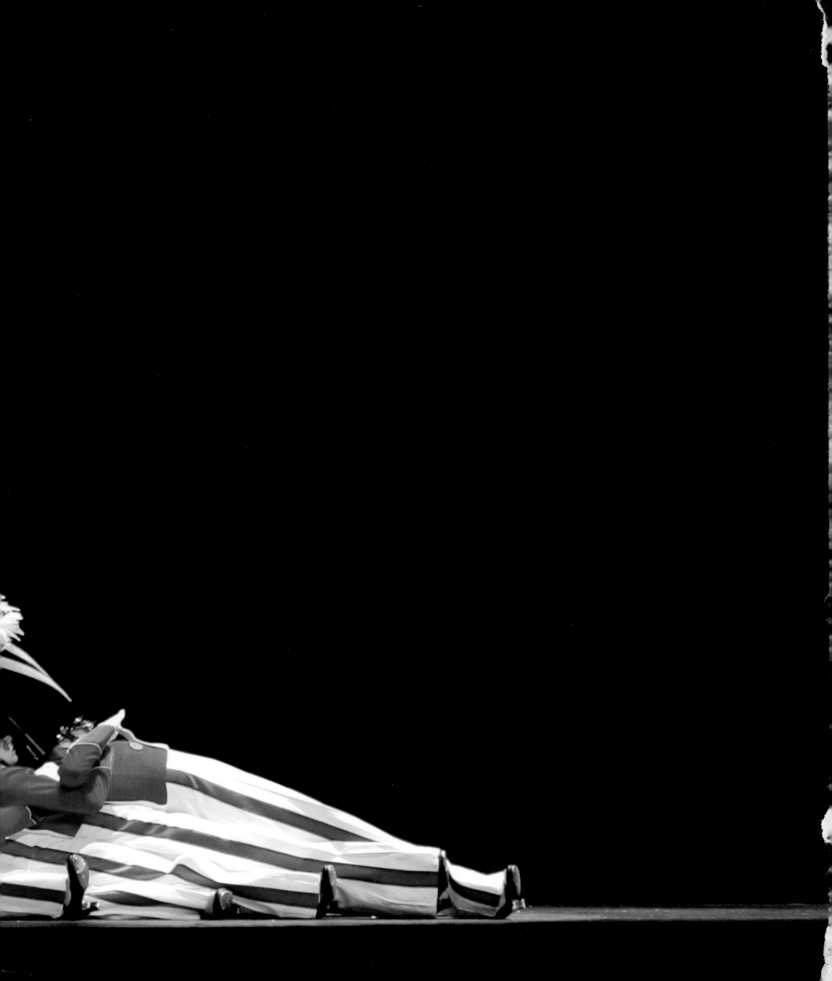

During the routine, no Rockette may bend her knees or turn her head in the slightest. The impressive execution of the sequence is accomplished in great part through the technique of guiding, which requires each Rockette to use her peripheral vision to look both down and to the side to make sure she is in line. The famous finale, where the 36 women fall backwards in slow motion like dominoes, is a delicate and physically demanding stunt.

"It takes a lot of strength and a lot of concentration," says director Linda Haberman. "By the time you get to the middle of the line, you have the weight of all those women coming at you." As the line falls, each woman must lock arms with the dancer in front of her, and staying stiff as a board, rock back on her heels to be caught by the Rockette behind her.

"The people in the middle of the line have to press forward to keep the whole line from going down really fast," explains Haberman. "When we first begin practicing the routine in rehearsals, we do it with just three people and then we keep adding until they build up to doing it with the whole line." (The final Rockette to fall is aided by a pillow to soften the blow.)

The dramatic finale, 1960.

SANTA CLAUS

Santa Claus, the embodiment of holiday cheer, is an essential part of the *Christmas Spectacular*. Mr. Claus has appeared in numerous *Christmas Spectaculars* throughout the show's history, boogying (in the popular "Santa's Gonna Rock and Roll"), rapping (in "Santa's Toy Fantasy"), and even joining a Rockette kick line. He now serves as the audience's guide through the 90-minute extravaganza.

Santa Claus gets a little affection from one of the Rockettes, 1967.

Several actors have had the honor of bringing Kris Kringle to life in the *Christmas Spectacular*, but it was in 1987 that Radio City's reigning Santa—who, when not dressed in his Santa reds, is known as actor Charles Edward Hall—joined the company.

A classically trained actor who hails from Kentucky, Hall feels he and Santa are virtually one and the same, after "working together" for so many years. Many are surprised to learn that Hall, the perfect Santa in looks, voice, and spirit onstage, is actually slight of frame and clean-shaven (he dons a fat suit, or "pod," as well as a beard, for the show). In fact, to prepare for the intense holiday production schedule, the actor increases his physical workouts to be fit enough to weather the demanding Christmas season schedule. (He also drinks 46 cases of Perrier during the show's run to stay hydrated.)

Hall's inspiration for his pitch-perfect Santa is his Uncle Walter, who used to make an appearance on Christmas Eve in Kris Kringle reds when the actor was a child.

"Everyone tells me I can do it till I get really old," he says. "And I hope to do it for the rest of my life. Santa's taught me to believe in the magic around me," says Hall, who describes performing at Radio City as "a dream."

BELOW: Santa, singing and dancing with the *Christmas Spectacular* ensemble, 1999. OPPOSITE: Charles Edward Hall has been performing as Santa at Radio City for more than 20 years and hopes to continue to play the jolly old man for many more.

Santa Claus performs with Mrs. Claus and the elves as they treat the audience to a tour of the North Pole, 1999.

THIS PAGE, CLOCKWISE FROM TOP LEFT: Santa welcomes audiences to Radio City, 2007; with his trusty elves, 1989; performing with friends, 1955. OPPOSITE: Santa shares a secret with the audience, 2007.

THE LIVING NATIVITY

With the exception of the Rockettes' whimsical "Parade of the Wooden Soldiers" routine, the only element of the *Radio City Christmas Spectacular* to return year after year is the majestic "Living Nativity." This moving depiction of the night of Christ's birth never fails to fill spectators with awe.

The "Living Nativity," 1966.

The "Living Nativity," has always captured the hearts of the audience with its celebration of the birth of Christ. The 1935 scene was simple and picturesque.

CLOCKWISE FROM TOP LEFT: The procession in the graduated choral staircase, 1946; the 1963 "Living Nativity;" Mary and Joseph with the Star of Bethlehem in the background, circa 1990s; the wisemen on horseback, 1946.

Much to the delight of adults and children alike, the "Living Nativity" always features live animals, which over the years have included camels, reindeers, donkeys, sheep, and horses. All of the animals take up residence at the Music Hall, in specially constructed stables, for the run of the show. When not performing in the *Christmas Spectacular*, the four-legged stars live on a 200-acre farm in upstate New York.

The sequence is not without its challenges: the substantial robes the Rockettes wear are heavy and hot, and while the animals are professionals, they are not housebroken.

But the end result is one of the most inspiring, special, and historic tableaus in live theater.

As Violet Homes, former Rockette director and choreographer, said, "The holiday season is especially moving for us, especially during the 'Living Nativity' segment, you feel very much in touch with the true meaning of Christmas. I think the audience reacts to the warmth we project onstage, that feeling of family. After all, we're not just 72 kicking legs."

The "Living Nativity," 2007.

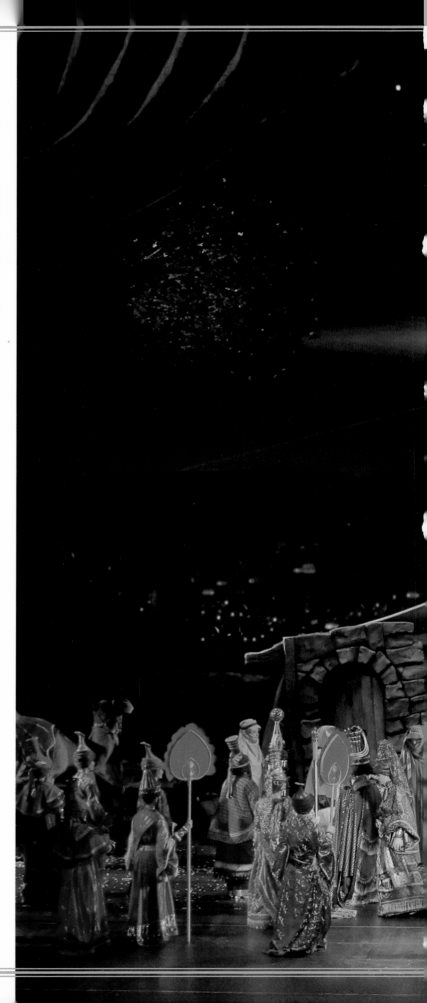

THE GRAND FINALE

After 90, glorious, nonstop minutes of holiday entertainment, the full cast of the *Radio City Christmas Spectacular* takes to the stage for a final bow. A magnificent moment, the finale allows audience members to applaud the efforts of every member of the show's cast, from Santa's elves to the Rockettes. Not surprisingly, these curtains calls are often met by standing ovations, a final thank-you to the performers for once again delivering a spectacular show.

The finale, 1948.

The *Radio City Christmas Spectacular* finale, 2007.

CHAPTER FOUR

THE LEGACY

OVER THE DECADES, more than 68 million people have celebrated the holidays with the *Radio City Christmas Spectacular*; more people see the production each year than any other live show in the United States.

It is not uncommon for a line of thousands, five people deep, to stretch down West 50th Street and around the block outside Radio City Music Hall once the holiday season begins. (The sight is so familiar it has even inspired a *New Yorker* magazine cartoon.) Visitors who don't secure a ticket to one performance wait in line to gain admittance to the next show. With the advent of the Internet, fans can order tickets online well in advance of the holiday season. To keep up with the demand, the *Radio City Christmas Spectacular* company performs up to six shows a day, every day, from 9:00 a.m. until 10:00 at night. In one season alone, the *Christmas Spectacular* takes place more than 205 times.

Thousands of people line the street waiting to see the *Christmas Spectacular* outside of Radio City Music Hall in New York, circa 1940s.

The spirit of the season surrounds Radio City guests long before they take their seats in the golden-lit auditorium. Over the years, decorations have included life-size wooden soldiers perched atop the Music Hall's neon-lit marquee and a soaring Christmas tree illuminated against the building's facade. Hundreds of yards of twinkle-lighted garlands adorn the Grand Foyer's railings, and a sparkling Christmas tree towers over guests in the lobby. A recent addition to the festive trimmings is a dazzling Christmas tree chandelier made of Swarovski crystals.

The crowds that flock to Radio City to see the show include a mix of visitors both young and old—lifetime New York residents, visitors from across the country, and tourists from around the world. For many, seeing the *Radio City Christmas Spectacular* once is just not enough. Countless fans return year after year, often handing down the holiday tradition to younger generations.

Perhaps the greatest, if not the most consistent, fan of the *Christmas Spectacular* is New Jersey resident Adam Medway, who at the age of six-and-a-half sat in the audience with his mother at the opening of Radio City Music Hall in 1932. He has returned to see the *Christmas Spectacular* every year since. He now attends the show with a group as large as 25 people that includes his wife and eight children—one of whom was born on Christmas Day. In more than 75 years, Medway has never seen the Rockettes make a mistake. (He used to watch for one, but now he's given up.)

"It really feels like Christmas when you see the show," he says. "You get the spirit of Christmas immediately. And when you walk out, you're just thrilled. The show is so dazzling."

Thousands of people wait in line at Rockefeller Center before the *Radio City Christmas Spectacular*, 1962. The famous Rockefeller Christmas Tree is in the background.

Like all great, enduring traditions, the *Radio City Christmas Spectacular* has both retained its essential spirit and evolved over its long history. What began as a variety show accompanying a major motion picture screening is now a singular entertainment extravaganza, showcasing one of the hardest working casts in show business, and the crown jewel of the Music Hall, the Radio City Rockettes.

Over the last century, theaters have opened and closed, and grand productions have come and gone, but Radio City, and its Christmas gift to the world, remains. The show unites generations and gains new fans every year. Each season, millions of visitors get the chance to spend time in a theater that retains it splendor from a bygone era while enjoying a show that continues to surprise and delight young and old.

"Parade of the Holidays" including the entire *Christmas Spectacular* cast, 1952.

From Russell Markert's innovative choreography to Leon Leonidoff's grand visions for the impressive stage, from the high-kicking Rockettes to the hard-working stagehands, many talented performers, directors, and designers have helped make the *Christmas Spectacular* an unforgettable experience for generations. Regardless of how Radio City's magnificent holiday production changes in the future—which it most certainly will—its millions of fans are guaranteed one thing for sure: true to its name, it will always be spectacular.

After more than seven decades of entertaining millions of people, the *Radio City Christmas Spectacular* is still as dazzling and exciting as it was when it first premiered in 1933. In 2007, the Rockettes kicked up their legs in Times Square.

The Rockettes have dazzled and delighted audiences both young and old for more than 75 years.

CREDITS AND ACKNOWLEDGMENTS

MSG ENTERTAINMENT WOULD LIKE TO THANK

the following people whose expertise and passion for the *Radio City Christmas Spectacular* enriched this book: Patrick Fahey, Set Designer; Linda Haberman, Director/Choreographer; Charles Hall, Santa; Jonathan Hochwald, Executive Vice President of Production; Kathy Hoovler, Production Stage Manager; Frank Krenz, Costume Designer; Barbara Van Zandt, Wardrobe Supervisor; Diane Jaust, Radio City Archivist; Stephanie Jacqueney, Legal; Kristina Heney, Marketing; Robynn Delin, Licensing & Merchandise.

MELCHER MEDIA WOULD LIKE TO THANK

David E. Brown, Francis Coy, Daniel del Valle, Liam Flanagan, Christopher Hampton, Coco Joly, Lauren Nathan, Jennifer Prestigiacomo, Holly Rothman, Jessi Rymill, Alex Tart, Shoshana Thaler, Rebecca Wiener, Betty Wong, and Megan Worman.